CW00375506

Understanding
Management
Gurus
in a week

BOB NORTON
CATHY SMITH

Hodder & Stoughton

A MEMBER OF THE HODDER HEADLINE GROUP

Acknowledgements:

Dale, Anthony, 'Daring to be Different', *Management Training*, February 1993

Downs, Alan, *Beyond the Looking Glass: Overcoming the Seductive Culture of Corporate Narcissism*, New York: American Management Association, 1997

Drucker, Peter, *The Concept of the Corporation*, New York: John Day, 1946

Drucker, Peter, *The Practice of Management*, London: Heinemann, 1955

Farnham, Alan, 'In Search of Suckers', *Fortune Magazine*, 14 October 1996

Ford, Henry, *My Life and Work*, London: Heinemann, 1922

Garvin, David A., 'Leveraging Processes for Strategic Advantage', *Harvard Business Review*, September–October 1995

Griffith, Victoria, 'It's a People Thing', *Financial Times*, 24 July 1997

Hammer, Michael, and Champy, James, *Re-engineering the Corporation*, London: Nicholas Brealey, 1993

Mintzberg, Henry, *Mintzberg on Management*, New York: Free Press, 1989

Moss Kanter, Rosabeth, *When Giants Learn to Dance*, London: Simon & Schuster, 1989

Ohmae, Kenichi, *The Mind of the Strategist: The Art of Japanese Management*, Harmondsworth: Penguin, 1982

Powell, Nik, 'How the Hell does Branson Manage it?', *Management Week*, July 1991

Schein, Edgar, *Organizational Psychology*, Englewood Cliffs NJ: Prentice Hall, 1980

Semler, Ricardo, *Maverick!*, London: Century, 1993

Sloan, Alfred, *My Years with General Motors*, Harmondsworth: Penguin, 1963

Willigan, Geraldine E., 'High-Performance Marketing: an interview with Nike's Phil Knight, *Harvard Business Review*, July–August 1992

Order queries: please contact Bookpoint Ltd, 39 Milton Park, Abingdon, Oxon OX14 4TD. Telephone: (44) 01235 400414, Fax: (44) 01235 400454. Lines are open from 9.00 - 6.00, Monday to Saturday, with a 24 hour message answering service. Email address: orders@bookpoint.co.uk

British Library Cataloguing in Publication Data
A catalogue record for this title is available from The British Library

ISBN 0 340 71173 6

First published 1998

Impression number	10	9	8	7	6	5	4	3	2	1
Year		2003	2002	2001	2000	1999	1998			

Cover photo from Comstock Photo Library.

Typeset by Multiplex Techniques Ltd, St Mary Cray, Kent.
Printed in Great Britain for Hodder & Stoughton Educational, a division of Hodder Headline Plc, 338 Euston Road, London NW1 3BH by Cox and Wyman, Reading, Berkshire.

the Institute
of Management

F O U N D A T I O N

The Institute of Management (IM) exists to promote the development, exercise and recognition of professional management. The Institute embraces all levels of management from student to chief executive and supports its own Foundation which provides a unique portfolio of services for all managers, enabling them to develop skills and achieve management excellence.

For information on the various levels and benefits of membership, please contact:

Department HS
Institute of Management
Cottingham Road
Corby
Northants NN17 1TT
Tel: 01536 204222
Fax: 01536 201651

This series is commissioned by the Institute of Management Foundation.

CONTENTS

■■INTRODUCTION■■

In Search of Excellence by Tom Peters and Robert Waterman
is one of the biggest management best-sellers of all time,
selling over 5 million copies worldwide. It is estimated,
however, that fewer than 10% of those copies were actually
read cover-to-cover. Whether that 10% made a significant
difference to the way those readers managed is difficult to
assess and impossible to quantify.

Peters' and Waterman's work on excellent companies was
the starting point for a huge surge of interest in
management throughout the 1980s. Gurus made a fortune
through writing, presenting and being consulted about
their ideas. The bubble burst somewhat in the mid-1990s,
partly because of strong reservations about the impact of
one of the most influential leading-edge ideas, business
process re-engineering, leading to a wave of cynicism about
the role of the gurus. There still appears, however, to be an
almost insatiable appetite for new ideas from managers and
a willingness on the part of gurus to supply them.

It is a good time, therefore, to ask whether the theorists
have provided clarification and direction or whether they
have served only to confuse and divert practising managers
from their main task. Do gurus burden our already
overcrowded time with outdated ideas from the past and
unestablished concepts of the present and future, or are
they significant in our ever-continuing effort to improve the
way that tasks, people and organisations are managed?

Understanding Management Gurus in a Week aims to answer
these questions by examining why the gurus are both
popular and criticised, by assessing the value we can get
from their writing, and by describing the key ideas, in brief

pen portraits, of those gurus who have made an impact on management thinking and development.

The thinkers and writers featured in this book have been selected by monitoring enquiries received in the Institute of Management's Information Centre, by trawling the views of Internet surfers and by surveying some of the principal business and management schools in the UK to discover the major influences on current management teaching. In this way, we attempt to focus on those thinkers who are of interest and importance to managers today.

Sunday	Management gurus – who are they?
Monday	The founding fathers of management
Tuesday	Leadership and strategy
Wednesday	Organisational change and the quality movement
Thursday	Learning
Friday	The next generation
Saturday	Getting value from the gurus

Management gurus – who are they?

'Oh, sure: It would be easy to make fun of gurus. So let's get started.'

Source: Alan Farnham, writing in *Fortune*, 14 October 1996.

At the end of the twentieth century, there is an obsession with management gurus – both with their ideas and with their shortcomings. Today we will consider their characteristics and what has made them so popular, while taking into account the comments of their critics. We shall ask:

- What is the significance of management theory?
- What is a management guru?
- Why are the gurus so popular?
- Why are the gurus criticised?

What is the significance of management theory?

In the mid-1990s, it became fashionable to knock management gurus. Articles like the one above in *Fortune* and books with titles such as *Fad Surfing in the Boardroom: Reclaiming the Courage to Manage in the Age of Instant Answers* started to appear.

There was reaction to the successive waves of ideas such as benchmarking, empowerment, portfolio working, quality function deployment and re-engineering which had begun to engulf all sectors of business, both private and public.

Such was the thirst for new ideas, that writers had even turned to historical figures such as Sun Tzu from the fourth century B.C. and his theories on the art of war.

The reaction against the gurus was also in protest at their material success at a time when their ideas had not always had beneficial effects on the organisations in which they had been implemented.

Even their detractors realised, however, that while one particular idea or programme is not the answer to a problem, not all of these ideas could be dismissed as fads, and that some of them were worthwhile. It was also recognised that in many cases it was not the fault of the gurus that their ideas were taken, and applied, out of context.

It is easy to become preoccupied with the ideas of today, forgetting that although the modern popularity of gurus can be traced back to 1982 and *In Search of Excellence*, there is a ragged line of management thinking which goes back over 100 years. At the centre of this stream of ideas was, and still is, the fundamental question which links the gurus together, for all that they have tried to tackle it in different ways: how can we best organise the resources at our disposal to get the job done at a price the customer will pay? Such a question was central to the work of Henry Ford in the early-twentieth-century American motor car factories, as it was to W. E. Deming in post-war Japan in the 1960s, and as it still is to Tom Peters addressing the global markets of today.

There are several major themes which can be traced back to the earlier days of management thinking and development.

1 An emphasis on systems, rules and work measurement, called Scientific Management, which has influenced management techniques and methods since the early days of the twentieth century, and whose major protagonist was F. W. Taylor.

2 A preoccupation with organisational form and structure, which extends back to Max Weber's classical bureaucracy and Henri Fayol's administrative management.

3 The growing discovery that people matter, that they are not cogs in a machine and that they should be recognised as individuals. This is commonly termed the Human Relations school, and it has now diversified into a myriad of theories and approaches.

The debate between scientific management and human relations management is far from won. Balancing the need for measurement and control with that of empowering people and giving them job satisfaction, continues to challenge the thinkers of today.

What is a management guru?

In general terms, a guru is a theorist or practitioner who has contributed to the development of management. Many people who fall into this category dislike the term 'guru'. Peter Drucker sees it as another word for 'charlatan', and Robert Blake (co-author of *The Managerial Grid*) thinks it 'puts an unprofessional stamp on things'. Rosabeth Moss Kanter prefers to be described as an educator and consultant: 'I'm a teacher, I have a job'. These reactions are unsurprising because although some commentators use the term guru respectfully, others, as we have seen, have used it in a dismissive, critical tone. The aversion to the label is also due to the fact that some dubious practitioners set themselves up as know-alls, whereas the more honest thinkers acknowledge their debt to those who have gone before and are prepared to listen in order to advance their thinking.

So how do we characterise a guru? They appear in a
number of guises:

1 *Pioneers* are the first to propose, or experiment with, a
   new approach. Such is the case with F. W. Taylor in the
   workshops of early-twentieth-century America, Elton
   Mayo with his discoveries on motivation at Hawthorne
   in the 1920s–1930s, Deming in post-war Japan and Reg
   Revans in the Belgium of the 1960s–1970s.

2 The earliest writers on management were *practitioners*
   who wanted to publicise their innovative and successful
   work. Alfred Sloan of General Motors and Henry Ford
   were practitioners whose achievements singled out
   themselves and their organisations as role models. Later,
   there was Thomas Watson of IBM and Michael Edwardes
   of British Leyland. Today, there is Anita Roddick of
   The Body Shop, John Harvey-Jones, formerly of ICI,
   Richard Branson of Virgin and Percy Barnevik, formerly
   of Asea Browne Boveri, in this 'practitioner' model of
   leader by example.

3 With the growth of information, many gurus, since the
   1950s, have been *professors*, reflecting the trends towards
   greater management research and providing the
   burgeoning 'science' of management with academic
   credibility. Mayo, Douglas McGregor and Rensis Likert
   developed their theories from a professorial base.
   Harvard continues to be one of the most productive and
   inspirational seats of learning, with Alfred Chandler,
   Michael Porter, Theodore Levitt, Rosabeth Moss Kanter
   and Robert Kaplan among the major contributors.

Almost without exception, the gurus have been writers,
prepared to share their theories or secrets of their successes.

In many cases, they are also lecturers, and even performers, in order to publicise their work. (Today, we think of Tom Peters, but F. W. Taylor worked hard to disseminate his views in the USA and the UK.) Where this work is complex, promotion has made the gurus' ideas more accessible to managers who may not have the time or the inclination to read academic books. Some of the most popular gurus today have also taken advantage of modern technology to market themselves, demonstrating their ideas on video and setting up Web sites. There has been a consistent trend towards their setting up their own consultancy firms.

Gurus need to be good communicators, using simple, powerful messages. In a world where we are bombarded with ideas and information in all aspects of our lives, there is intense competition for our attention. Slogans such as 'Quality is free' (Philip Crosby), 'Stick to the knitting' (Peters and Waterman) and 'Managers do things right, leaders do the right thing' (Warren Bennis) help to get the message over.

Gurus may have fresh, original ideas, but equally they may popularise and build on the work of earlier writers. Tom Peters is not slow to acknowledge the influence of previous thinkers: Bennis and his research into the nature of leadership, McGregor with his now famous Theory X and Theory Y, and Peter Drucker writing over a period spanning more than 50 years. In his turn, Drucker says that it all really started with Taylor and the principles of Scientific Management.

Some gurus, like Charles Handy, are able to keep coming up with new ideas on a grand scale across the broad

spectrum of management. Others such as R. Meredith
Belbin (team role theory), Reg Revans (action learning) and
Edward de Bono (lateral thinking), have become famous on
the strength of one enduring theory or model which has
been refined and extended over time.

Gurus, by definition, must have followers, and today they
must also become known internationally to be successful.
Most gurus have been American; this is usually attributed
to the fact that Americans are particularly receptive to new
ideas. In the last couple of decades, there has been a growing
interest in Japanese management which has redressed the
balance a little. There are very few gurus from Asia,
however. Asian managers and organisations seem successful
enough without them.

Why are the gurus so popular?

There are a number of reasons for the rise of the
management gurus:

1 Managers who are increasingly pressed for time
   welcome relatively quick and easy solutions to the often
   complex and difficult problems and situations which
   they face. In times of rapid change (such change
   prompted in part by the writings of the gurus
   themselves, according to the cynics), they seek help and
   advice that will assist them in making sense of the
   environment in which they are working. Gurus offer a
   measure of assurance and advice on how to understand
   and take control of a situation.
2 Managers sometimes lack confidence in their own
   judgement and listen to ideas or prophecies because they

can't be sure that they won't work or lead to success. In complex times, new (or even apparently new) thoughts or ideas may prove difficult to resist.

3   There is a natural fear on the part of managers that if they don't take notice of emerging management theories, they will get left behind. As individuals, they may fail to keep up with their peers; their companies may fail to achieve and maintain an advantage over their competitors; and their country or region may get overtaken by another.

4   Gurus recognise and understand managers' needs and concerns. Managers, like colleagues in some other professions, can have feelings of insecurity about the worth of their role and their status. Gurus appeal to managers' need for self-esteem by promoting the importance of the manager's place in society.

Why are the gurus criticised?

These are some of the charges levelled against the gurus:

1   *There are inherent contradictions in what they say* when they are seen as a group dispensing advice. For example, total quality management, which is now embedded into the culture of management, takes time to achieve, with its emphasis on continuous improvement and zero defects. In the competitive environment of the 1990s, however, managers are advised that speed to market is at a premium. Similarly, achieving a *customer focus*, another buzzword term, lays increasing emphasis on the need for loyal, long-serving employees, whereas re-engineering and flexible working have led to slimmer workforces.

2   *Their work is not always academically rigorous.* Some gurus
    such as Michael Porter seem to be fireproof: even the
    gurus' harshest critics do not question the academic
    basis of his work; and Rosabeth Moss Kanter has been
    praised for the thoughtfulness and complexity of her
    contribution. Others, however, such as Abraham Maslow
    and R. Meredith Belbin, have had the validity of their
    research findings questioned by academics, popular
    though their work is with managers.

3   *They can be arrogant,* thinking that their ideas are the best
    and cannot be altered or influenced by others, and to a
    certain extent, they can't practise what they preach. For
    example, Rosabeth Moss Kanter was heavily criticised
    when she took over as editor of the *Harvard Business
    Review,* for being too authoritarian. One manager said of
    Deming, 'He was a nonstop lecturer .... always trying to
    shove his ideas down your throat'. On the other hand,
    where gurus do allow or accept that others can modify
    and extend their work, it has strengthened their theory
    and consolidated their reputation. For example, the
    findings of Geert Hofstede on cultural diversity have

been built upon by many other researchers who acknowledge their debt.

4 *They change their tune.* Tom Peters has been criticised for saying that there are no excellent companies five years after he quoted American examples in *In Search of Excellence.* Charles Handy's later thinking seems to turn the earlier assertions of *Understanding Organizations* upside down. On the other hand, although self-contradiction can lead to the questioning of a guru's integrity, development and progression of thinking to adapt to changing times is essential. Tom Peters trumpets his own inconsistency, and just as often as he has changed his mind, he manages to touch a raw nerve.

5 *Their ideas don't work.* There are plenty of examples where a guru's idea has been implemented with little success, such as with Frederick Herzberg's concept of job enrichment, or where it has received a mixed reception, such as with Michael Hammer and James Champy's re-engineering.

6 *They are only interested in making money.* It is true that some gurus like Tom Peters have got rich through the lecture circuit; and others such as Charles Handy and Ricardo Semler charge high fees in an effort to try to control the number of seminar appearances, or just refuse requests, preferring to follow other activities.

Summary

Today, we have looked at the phenomenon of management gurus and at their widespread appeal – and limitations. During the rest of the week, we will consider what they have said and how much influence they have had. We start tomorrow with the founding fathers of management thinking.

The founding fathers of management

The consideration of management as an activity in its own right hardly existed 100 years ago. During the first half of the twentieth century, however, the work of a number of management gurus laid the foundations of management as we know it today. Although the ideas of these gurus have been developed by later writers, they are significant because they represent the beginnings of management. In those early years, there was at first an emphasis on task- or organisation-based efficiency, followed by the discovery that effectiveness also comes from an understanding of the people involved. This research highlighted the need to reconcile people with systems and vice versa – an issue addressed by Peter Drucker who sought a balance between the two. Today, we will look at the ideas of:

- Frederick Taylor
- Henri Fayol
- Max Weber
- Elton Mayo
- Douglas McGregor
- Abraham Maslow
- Frederick Herzberg
- Peter Drucker

Frederick Winslow Taylor – Scientific Management

Although Peter Drucker is often referred to as the guru's guru, Drucker himself suggests that this accolade should be given to F. W. Taylor (1856–1917). Taylor's ideas were based on his work in American industry, and they involve four main principles:

1 Each part of an individual's work should be analysed in minute detail in order to devise the most efficient method for undertaking the job.
2 The most suitable person to undertake the job should be chosen and taught to do the job in the exact way devised.
3 Managers should cooperate with workers to ensure that the job is done in the best way.
4 There must be a clear division of work and responsibility between management and workers: managers plan and supervise work; workers carry it out.

Taylor's main motivation was to increase productivity so that workers could earn decent pay. His approach was adopted by Henry Ford in the latter's development of mass production techniques. More recently, several management techniques have come to the fore, such as quality systems, re-engineering and benchmarking, whose methods can be traced back to Taylor. The main objection to what became known as Taylorism, is that it degenerated into an inhumane and mechanistic approach to working, treating people like machines rather than as human beings who need to be motivated. Taylor's legacy, however, is that he

was the first person to think about the activity of
management in an age that put a premium on technical
knowledge.

Key text: *The Principles of Scientific Management*, 1911.

Frederick Taylor's theories were put into effect by Henry Ford who
created the first mass production line. In *My Life and Work* (1922),
Ford stated that 'by the aid of scientific study one man is able to do
somewhat more than four did only a comparatively few years ago.
That [moving] line established the efficiency of the method and we
now use it everywhere. The assembling of the motor, formerly done
by one man, is now divided into eighty-four operations'. Ford,
following Taylor, believed that 'if [the workman] makes an honest,
wholehearted investment, high wages ought to be his reward. Not
only has he earned them, but he has had a big part in creating them.'

Henri Fayol – Functionalism

Henri Fayol (1841–1925) spent his entire career with one
company, the French mining and metallurgical combine
Commentary-Fourchamboult-Decazeville. Labelled the
founding father of the administration school, he was the
first European to consider the activities of management,
and, unlike Taylor, he took a top-down approach. His ideas
were first published in 1916 but only gained widespread
recognition when they appeared in translation in 1949.

Fayol divided all organisational activities into six functions:
technical, commercial, financial, security, accounting and
managerial. The managerial function acts as an umbrella
activity to the others and consists of five activities: planning,
organising, coordinating, commanding and controlling.

Fayol also established 14 general principles of management which lend definition, description and technique to the five-point approach. These include: division of work; authority and responsibility; discipline; unity of command; unity of direction; subordination of individual interest to general interest; remuneration; centralisation; line of authority and stability of tenure.

Amongst the contemporaries influenced by Fayol was Alfred Sloan of General Motors. Subsequently, however, Fayol has been criticised on a number of counts: weak analysis, a confusion of structure with process, and an over-reliance on top-down bureaucracy. His achievement, nonetheless, was to identify management as a process and to lay out a series of principles to make best use of people. Furthermore, he believed that management could and should be taught – a revolutionary idea at the time. Practising managers can still identify the main elements of their work in Fayol's system, prescriptive though it may seem today.

Key text: *General and Industrial Management*, translated by Constance Storrs, 1949.

At General Motors in the 1920s and 1930s, Alfred Sloan put into practice Henri Fayol's ideas, creating a decentralised, divisionalised structure with coordinated central policy control. This enabled Sloan to use the organisation's size without making it cumbersome and to turn General Motors into the biggest company in the world. In *My Years with General Motors* (1963), Sloan claimed that 'we recognized the problems and thought more in terms of organizational principles and philosophies than did most businessmen of that time. The principles of organization got more attention among us than they did then in all the universities.'

Max Weber – Bureaucracy

Max Weber (1864–1920), a German sociologist who studied power and authority in organisations, proposed the concept of *bureaucracy* as the most efficient form of administration. Whereas Taylor had studied the way work was carried out, Weber created a series of rules by which an organisation could function. He outlined the roles of job holders within a hierarchy where candidates were appointed on merit and were subject to the rules of the organisation. He suggested that each part of the organisation should have a clearly defined area of specialisation and that management should be impartial and impersonal, and every employee should be treated equally. He distinguished different types of authority: traditional, charismatic and legal.

In modern times, bureaucracy has almost turned into a term of abuse, standing for red tape and inflexible management. Although approaches to organisation structure changed radically in the 1980s, bureaucracy continues to have a strong influence.

Key text: *The Theory of Social and Economic Organization*, 1924, translated 1947.

Elton Mayo – The Hawthorne Experiments

Elton Mayo (1880–1949) was an Australian by birth but his significant work was carried out while he was a professor at Harvard in the USA. In the 1920s, he was invited to join the experiments on efficiency being carried out at the Hawthorne plant of Western Electric.

One series of experiments found not only that productivity went up within a group as various incentives were tried out – altering lighting levels, the length of rest pauses and varying financial incentives – but also that it went up whether the incentive was increased or decreased! A parallel series revealed that, whatever the incentive, the group showed a resistance to it and developed its own ethos and identity which was counter-productive.

I'VE SWITCHED OFF ALL THE LIGHTS, BUT THEY STILL WON'T GO HOME!

Mayo concluded that the difference between the two groups was to be found in the type of supervision for each group. Where the supervisor encouraged participation and got to know the operators, an *esprit de corps* grew up within the group and output increased. He noted that:

- Job satisfaction increased as workers were given more freedom to determine their working conditions and to set their own standards of output
- Job satisfaction and output depended more on cooperation and on a feeling of worth than on physical working conditions

Mayo has been hailed as one of the fathers of personnel management. His interpretation of the evidence gathered at Hawthorne lay the foundations of the Human Relations school by arguing that the way people are managed can be crucial to a firm's economic success. Mayo offered not necessarily an alternative to Taylor's scientific management, understanding that the production side of business management could never be sidelined, but rather an approach which Taylorites could not ignore.

Key text: *The Human Problems of an Industrial Civilization*, 1933.

Douglas McGregor – Theory X and Theory Y

Douglas McGregor (1906–1964), a social psychologist, was Professor of Management at Massachusetts Institute of Technology. McGregor suggested that managers' behaviour is influenced by their assumptions about the people under their leadership.

Managers who have a *Theory X* attitude have a traditional view of direction and control. They assume that people are indifferent to organisational objectives, will avoid responsibility and prefer to be directed, actively dislike work, will avoid it wherever possible and see money and security as the only reasons for working harder. A Theory X management style, following Taylor, therefore requires close, firm supervision with clearly specified tasks and the threat of punishment or the promise of greater pay as the motivators. Managers with a *Theory Y* view, on the other hand, assume that people will work towards organisational objectives if they see personal gain in doing so, will accept, and even seek, responsibility and can direct themselves when they share objectives with the organisation. A Theory Y management style, following Mayo, establishes a cooperative environment in which the needs of both organisation and individual can be met.

WHAT DO YOU MEAN, THEY'VE WORKED HARDER WHILE YOU WERE ON HOLIDAY

Although Theory X and Theory Y were criticised for being too polarised, McGregor did not regard them as rigid approaches. He was one of the first to argue that leadership was more about the relationship between the leader and the situation they faced, rather than merely about the characteristics of the leader alone.

Key text: *The Human Side of Enterprise*, 1960

Abraham Maslow - The Hierarchy of Needs

Abraham Maslow (1908-1970) was also an American psychologist who was initially a supporter of Theory Y until he saw it put into practice in an electronics company. His criticism of it was that it was too *laissez-faire*, arguing that everyone requires security and reassurance.

Maslow's own theory was that human needs can be viewed as a hierarchy, ascending from the lowest to the highest. When one set of needs is satisfied, it is no longer a motivator; motivation is then generated by the unsatisfied needs. The hierarchy of needs is usually represented as a pyramid, although Maslow himself did not present it in this way.

1 *Survival or physiological needs:* the most primitive of all animal needs, such as food and water, shelter and warmth, and sleep.
2 *Security or safety needs:* in early times, this was a desire to be free of physical danger, but nowadays it is felt in social and financial, rather than physical, terms.
3 *Social needs:* to belong and to be accepted by others.
4 *Ego-status needs:* to be held in esteem by oneself and by others, a need which is satisfied by power, prestige and self-confidence.
5 *Self-fulfilment needs:* to maximise one's skills and talents in achievement.

Academics have found little evidence to support Maslow's theory, but it influenced other thinkers and it continues to strike a chord with practising managers. Maslow's theory takes a holistic view, being an explanation of human behaviour in general, not just in the workplace. This makes it important to managers who recognise that life outside work impinges on performance at work.

Key text: *Motivation and Personality*, 1954.

Frederick Herzberg – The Hygiene-Motivation Theory

Frederick Herzberg (b. 1923) is a psychologist who became Professor of Management at Utah University. In his own words, he had 'an overriding interest in mental health' which led to the development of his hygiene-motivation theory.

Herzberg suggested that the time-honoured management practice of giving employees a figurative kick in the ass (KITA) was not effective as a means of motivation.

Nor indeed was improving factors in the context or environment in which they work, such as pay and benefits, working conditions and hours, supervision and other working relationships. He termed these factors *hygiene factors* because they do not in themselves promote job satisfaction, but serve primarily to prevent job dissatisfaction, just as good hygiene does not in itself produce good health although lack of it will cause disease. *Motivators*, on the other hand, relate to what a person does at work rather than to the context in which it is done. These lead to job satisfaction and include achievement, recognition, responsibility or advancement. The two sets of factors are separate and distinct; they are not opposites.

Herzberg's theory is not highly regarded by psychologists today, but practising managers have found that it provides useful guidelines. Herzberg's greatest contribution is the knowledge that motivation comes from within the individual: it cannot be imposed by an organisation according to a formula.

Key text: *The Motivation to Work*, 1959.

Peter Drucker – The Man Who Discovered Management

Peter Drucker (b. 1909) is without question the most significant management guru of the twentieth century. His central message is about the importance of management in society. Drucker was an Austrian who emigrated to the USA in 1937 where he later became Professor of Management at New York University and subsequently at the Claremont Graduate School in Claremont, California. He has been a prolific writer on diverse management topics.

In *The Practice of Management* (1955), Drucker established five basic roles of management: to set objectives; to organise; to motivate and communicate; to measure; and to develop people. He also invented the term *management by objectives*, stating that 'a manager's job should be based on a task to be performed in order to obtain the company's objectives'.

Many of the themes of modern management thinking first appeared in Drucker's writing. For example, in *The Concept of the Corporation* (1946), he was the first to suggest that the firm (in this case, General Motors) was a social as much as an economic organisation. He also foreshadowed the empowerment of workers, arguing that the assembly line removed people's opportunity to be engaged in their job and to be proud of the product they were manufacturing. Similarly, he was the first to emphasise the importance of marketing, writing that 'there is only one valid definition of business purpose: to create a customer.' Later, in *The Age of Discontinuity* (1969), he anticipated the work of Charles Handy and the rise of the *knowledge economy*, and has since developed this theme, looking at the impact on managers of the rise of the *knowledge worker*.

Drucker has been criticised for inconsistencies in his work, although these are inevitable in a career which has spanned 60 years. For example, his focus, once on large organisations, later shifted to small business. He has upbraided himself for being 10 years premature with his forecasts, but his reputation rests not only on his ability as a management theorist but also on pioneering philosophies that today are accepted by all.

Key texts: *The Practice of Management*, 1954;
The Age of Discontinuity, 1969.

Summary

Today, we have looked at the ideas of those early writers who were concerned primarily with efficiency, of those who stressed the importance of human motives, and of Peter Drucker who sought to reconcile the two. Pre-Drucker, the ideas of the pioneers seem simplistic, perhaps obvious today. They formed, however, the basis of today's thinking, approaches and explorations. Tomorrow, we will start considering modern-day gurus, beginning with those who have focused on strategy and leadership.

Leadership and strategy

Until the Second World War, leadership and strategy were
terms principally applied to political and military matters.
The war itself produced such an intensity of thinking about
how to win that, post-war, management thinkers on both
sides of the Atlantic began to suggest that the concepts and
approaches applied to war might also be profitably applied
to business and industry. Since then, the questions of
leadership and strategy have increasingly preoccupied the
gurus. Today, we shall look firstly at writers on leadership
and secondly at writers on strategy.

1 *Leadership:*

- Rensis Likert
- Robert Blake and Jane Mouton
- John Adair
- Warren Bennis
- John Kotter

2 *Strategy:*

- Alfred D. Chandler and Igor Ansoff
- Henry Mintzberg
- Michael Porter
- Theodore Levitt
- Kenichi Ohmae
- Gary Hamel and C. K. Prahalad

Leadership

Leadership continues to be something of the Holy Grail of management thinking: find the key to leadership and the door to success will be opened. Drucker has said that leadership can, and must, be learned. This has not proved easy. Writers in all ages have focused on the qualities and characteristics of 'Great People' in the hope that, if they may be identified, then they may be emulated. Victories in battle, successes in business and, more recently, in sport, have provided models to emulate. Other approaches have focused on situational research, on the definition of the functions, tasks and roles of leaders, and on the differences between managers and leaders.

Rensis Likert – System 4

Rensis Likert (1903–1981) was a Professor at the Institute for Social Research, University of Michigan. His work concentrated on situational leadership research – how behaviour adapts to take account of people *and* of the situation facing the leader. Likert established four systems of management to interpret the way managers behave towards others, depending on the situation:

- *System 1: Exploitive/Authoritative* – where management controls subordinates through fear and threats ('Do as I say')
- *System 2: Benevolent/Authoritative* – where subordinate attitudes are subservient to superiors, management uses rewards, and decisions are taken at the top ('You should do as I say because it's good for you')

- *System 3: Consultative* – where some involvement is sought but management still basically extracts only what it wants to hear ('I hear what you say ....')
- *System 4: Participative* – where management makes full use of group involvement, and decision-making is widespread and integrated ('How shall we tackle this?')

Likert's System 4 focuses on developing people to attain high levels of job satisfaction through full participation and, like McGregor's theories, it helped to lay the groundwork for the empowering style of the 1990s. But Likert did not prescribe System 4 to the exclusion of the other three. The approach you adopt depends on the situation, and a situational approach may require different kinds of leadership for different tasks and activities.

Key text: *New Patterns of Management*, 1961.

Robert Blake and Jane Mouton – The Managerial Grid

Robert Blake (b. 1918) and Jane Mouton (1930-1987) were psychologists based at the University of Texas. Like McGregor and Likert, they started with the assumption that the manager's job is to get things done by nurturing attitudes and behaviour which lead to better performance, learning and a sense of satisfaction from participating in achievement. Blake and Mouton argued that all management is composed fundamentally of the interaction between a manager's concern for getting the task done, on the one hand, and concern for the people who do it on the other. Taylor's task-based drive for efficiency and Fayol's hierarchical command and control structure can lead to treating people like cogs in a machine. On the other hand, if avoidance of conflict and an overriding concern for generating good fellowship predominate, then production will suffer and getting things done will become incidental.

Blake and Mouton established The Managerial Grid with two matrices: concern for task and concern for people – graded 1 to 9. A 9.1 manager – one too preoccupied with task – is in danger of becoming a slave-driver; a 1.9 manager – one too concerned for people – becomes a 'country-club' manager. The ideal target to aim for is the 9.9 manager who integrates production and human requirements in a team approach by developing the team players to get things done. Blake's and Mouton's Managerial Grid and their phased programme of organisational development has been applied successfully in North America, Asia and Europe.

Key text: *The Managerial Grid*, 1964.

John Adair – Action-Centered Leadership

John Adair (b. 1934) is Professor of Leadership Studies at the University of Surrey, and has drawn on his extensive military experience and work at Sandhurst in identifying not two, but three fundamental concerns for managers to look after at the same time:

1 *Task needs* – with implications for the actions and behaviours required to tackle objectives.
2 *Individual needs* – getting people to feel part of the group so that they can offer their maximum contribution.
3 *Team needs* – maintaining and developing the cohesion and motivation of the group to focus constructively on tasks.

Adair defines the major functions that leaders need to carry out to meet these needs:

- *Planning:* defining goals and tasks, making practical plans
- *Informing:* clarifying goals and tasks, sharing information
- *Initiating:* briefing groups, explaining why, allocating tasks
- *Supporting:* encouraging (and disciplining) groups and individuals, creating team spirit, reconciling disagreements
- *Controlling:* setting and maintaining standards, influencing pace and direction
- *Evaluating:* checking and testing progress, and helping the group to evaluate its own performance

Key texts: *Action-centered Leadership*, 1973; *Understanding Motivation*, 1990.

Warren Bennis – 'Managers do Things Right, Leaders do the Right Thing'

Warren Bennis (b. 1925), Professor of Management at the University of Southern California, is a widely recognised leadership expert who acknowledges the influence of earlier writers on his thinking – particularly McGregor. In turn, Bennis has influenced Peters, Waterman and many others.

In 1977, Abraham Zaleznik, Professor of the Social Psychology of Management at Harvard, wrote a landmark article in *Harvard Business Review* (May–June 1977) entitled 'Managers and leaders – are they different?' Zaleznik's article stimulated widespread interest and was a contributory factor in Bennis carrying out extensive research in the USA into common leadership factors. Bennis identified a number of elements commonly found in effective leaders. Leaders:

- Attend to vision and the longer-term, not just the immediate bottom-line
- Originate and innovate with an eye always on the horizon
- Are good communicators, often using metaphor, analogy and vivid illustration
- Earn and generate trust which binds leader and followers together
- Have integrity – an honest self-awareness about themselves
- Challenge assumptions by asking why in preference to how or when
- Have a commitment to learning as a crucial element in the process of change
- Expect the best of people around them but are realistic about expectations
- Have a passion and a contagious enthusiasm for what they are doing
- Show daring – a penchant for trying out new things and taking risks
- Have strong, successful family ties

Bennis, like Drucker, believes that leadership can be learned.

Key text: *On Becoming a Leader*, 1989.

> *'His major ability is leadership, his ability to inspire and motivate. He is*
> *obviously different from other people, more outwardly relaxed in the way*
> *he presents himself. You gain his trust by delivering. He is able to choose*
> *people correctly in the first place, often on very little experience and then*
> *to work with them successfully.'*
>
> *Source:* Nik Powell describing his former partner Richard Branson in
> 'How the hell does Branson manage it?', *Management Week,* July 1991.

John Kotter – Leadership Produces Change

John Kotter (b. 1947) is Professor of Organisational
Behaviour and Human Resource Management at Harvard
Business School. For Kotter, leaders are born, then made.
Kotter stresses that the main function of leadership is to
change both *how* things are done and, indeed, *what* things
are done. This is achieved through three functions that the
leader must perform.

1 *Establish direction:* it is the leader's role to develop
both a vision for the future and strategies for
change which will help to realise that vision.
2 *Align people:* through effective communication,
the leader must influence the development of teams
so as to ensure that the vision and strategies are
understood.
3 *Motivate and inspire:* the leader must energise
people to move in the right direction, to give of their
best and to overcome obstacles to change by
understanding and appealing to their motives.

With Kotter, we begin to see the emergence of the leader as enabler and facilitator. Kotter believes that leaders appear to thrive on achieving, and on influencing others to achieve.

Kotter's most recent work explores the leadership of Matsushita of Japan whom he describes as the most remarkable entrepreneur of the twentieth century.

As we see above, Kotter also places emphasis on the leader's role in strategy formulation, which is where we turn next.

Key text: *A Force for Change*, 1990.

Strategy

Although it might appear that strategy is a sophisticated and detailed business, today we see that the gurus themselves come down against unnecessary complexity.

Alfred D. Chandler and Igor Ansoff – Pioneers in Strategy

In the first half of the twentieth century, there was a pervasive emphasis on how things were done, on how resources were organised. It was in the early 1960s that the academics Alfred D. Chandler (b. 1918) and Igor Ansoff (b. 1918) proposed alternative options to this approach, and they have had a profound effect on later writers.

Chandler, a business historian at Harvard, argued that the major function of an organisation was to implement strategy. The optimum use of resources therefore stemmed not merely from the way they were organised but more importantly from what the organisation was trying to achieve: its strategic goals. This has been expressed more succinctly as 'Structure follows strategy'.

In contrast, Ansoff argued that the best potential for meeting objectives lay firstly with producing the optimum resource allocation and then by matching business opportunities with organisational resources. The core of Ansoff's approach to corporate strategy lay with maximising strengths and minimising weaknesses. He acknowledged that while this could help an organisation to grow strong, it could also make it too rigid and slow to adapt to change – he called this 'paralysis by analysis'. His subsequent work was therefore a search for flexibility in strategic planning and positioning, and was based on the understanding that strategy formulation will invariably be based on incomplete and uncertain information.

Ultimately, for Ansoff, universal prescriptions don't work. The organisation has to devise its own flexible solutions, and these are to be found in the way the organisation learns and interacts with the changing environment.

Key texts: Chandler – *Strategy and Structure*, 1962; Ansoff – *Corporate Strategy*, 1965.

Henry Mintzberg – The Rise and Fall of Strategic Planning

Getting to grips with change has also dominated Henry Mintzberg's thinking on strategy. Mintzberg (b. 1939), a Professor at McGill University in Montreal, initially came to prominence as a result of researching what managers did – how they actually spent their time.

Mintzberg said that managing strategy was not so much about promoting change as about knowing when to do so. Rolling five-year plans often became mechanical, consumed with repetitive processes. This has the effect of unconsciously programming organisations into fixed patterns. In *Mintzberg On Management*, he said:

'The real challenge in crafting strategy lies in detecting the subtle discontinuities that may undermine an organisation in the future. And for that, there is no technique, no program, just a sharp mind in touch with the situation. Such discontinuities are unexpected and irregular, essentially unprecedented. They can be dealt with only by minds that are attuned to existing patterns yet able to perceive important breaks in them.'

Key texts: *Mintzberg on Management*, 1989; *The Rise and Fall of Strategic Planning*, 1994.

Michael Porter – Competitive Advantage

One of the key contributions to shaping and reshaping thinking in the age of competition is Michael Porter's book *Competitive Strategy* which expounded techniques for analysing industries and competitors.

Porter (b. 1947), a Professor at Harvard, starts neither with change nor with organisational structure but with profitability as the strategic driver. He argues that there are five competitive forces which determine industry profitability:

1 The potential of new entrants into the industry.
2 The bargaining power of customers.
3 The threat of substitute products.
4 The bargaining power of suppliers.
5 The activities of existing competitors.

One of the most important concepts established by Porter is that of the Value Chain: a systematic way of examining all the activities a firm performs and how these interact. Primary activities are inbound logistics, outbound logistics, marketing, sales and service. Support activities are procurement, technology development, human resource management, and infrastructure. The way that one activity in the chain interacts with another can be crucial; this can occur within the organisation, or externally with suppliers or partners.

Porter argues that a firm gains competitive advantage by performing these activities – alone or linked – more cheaply, or in a better way, than its competitors. Porter's influence has been profound and has implications, like the work of Ansoff and Mintzberg above, for organisation structure, which we look at tomorrow.

Key texts: *Competitive Strategy: Techniques for Analysing Industries and Competitors*, 1980; *Competitive Advantage: Creating and Sustaining Superior Performance*, 1985.

Theodore Levitt – Marketing Myopia

A Professor at Harvard and once editor of *Harvard Business Review,* Theodore Levitt (b. 1925) has been hailed as the father of marketing strategy. In one landmark journal article, published in *Harvard Business Review* in 1960, he transformed the way companies viewed their business. He criticised the American railroad industry for not understanding that it was principally in the business of transport rather than merely the railway business. His argument was that industry is not necessarily a goods-producing process but rather a customer-satisfying process.

Levitt argued – as did Mintzberg – against a rigid planning process and for thinking boldly about deceptively simple questions such as:

- What business are we in?
- Who are our customers?
- What are we trying to achieve?
- Why do we do things like this?

For Levitt, marketing consists of efforts to discover, create, arouse and satisfy customer needs. In the 1980s, as the world shrank with cheaper travel and telecommunications, Levitt argued in favour of the concept of global marketing. This is territory which Kenichi Ohmae has since made his own.

Key texts: 'Marketing Myopia', *Harvard Business Review,* July–August 1960; *Marketing Imagination,* 1983.

Kenichi Ohmae – Triad Power and the Global Village

A Consultant with McKinsey, Kenichi Ohmae (b. 1943) opens a door on Japan and the East for Westerners; and for the Japanese, it is the reverse: he bridges East and West. Ohmae came to prominence as the writer of *Triad Power* which held that the key to success was for companies to have a foothold in each of the world's three main markets: the USA, the Japanese–Pacific Rim and Europe. Without this three-pronged approach, companies are susceptible to attack from competitors.

Ohmae, like Ansoff and Mintzberg, makes a persuasive case for disposing of rational models of systems planning and analysis, arguing that they do not fit the real world. In *The Mind of the Strategist*, he describes how the successful competitive strategies of the Japanese are practised instinctively by managers who have had no training in formal techniques. He advocates the continuous application of imagination, and training in logical thought processes:

'The strategist's method is very simply to challenge the prevailing assumptions with a single question – why? – and to put the same question relentlessly to those responsible for the current way of doing things until they are sick of it'.

Key texts: *The Mind of the Strategist: the Art of Japanese Management,* 1982; *Triad Power: the Coming Shape of Global Competition;* 1985; *The Borderless World: Power and Strategy in the Interlinked Economy,* 1992.

Gary Hamel and C. K. Prahalad – Core Competence

Gary Hamel is visiting Professor of Strategic and International Management at London Business School. C. K. Prahalad is Professor of Business Administration at the University of Michigan's Graduate School of Business

Administration. Together they have set up a consultancy firm which advises on their area of expertise: strategy.

Hamel and Prahalad have coined the term *core competencies*. They define these as 'the collective learning in the organization'. The concept of core competencies looks at the organisation not as a portfolio of products and services, but as a system of activities, some of which are more critical than others. The organisation can reach a position of competitive strength by analysing what it is that it does that is better than what others can do. Core competencies should make a substantial contribution to perceived customer benefits, be difficult to imitate, and provide access to a wide variety of markets.

In spite of the undoubted importance of the concept, many organisations have experienced problems in identifying their core competencies. Hamel believes that this is because people are often less than rigorous in defining their core competencies and because they try to identify them in a mechanistic rather than a creative way. In his view, strategy is emotional as well as analytical. Hamel and Prahalad urge a new approach to strategy where the key components are growth, transformation, imagination, breaking the rules, and democratisation of the strategic process. This perspective is necessary in an age where the onus is on transforming not just individual companies but also entire industries.

Key texts: 'The Core Competence of the Corporation', *Harvard Business Review*, May–June 1990; *Competing for the Future*, 1994.

'We can now see that the entire industry has gone through a major shift. But I'm happy to say that we pretty much led the charge by being the first to understand the importance of the brand and the consumer. … We came to see that focusing solely on the product was a great way for a brand to start, but it just wasn't enough. We had to fill in the blanks. We had to learn to do well all the things involved in getting to the consumer, starting with understanding who the consumer is and what the brand represents. .... We used to think that everything started in the lab. Now we realise that everything spins off the consumer.'

Source: Phil Knight, founder, chairman and CEO of Nike, quoted in 'High-Performance Marketing: an interview with Nike's Phil Knight', Geraldine E Willigan, *Harvard Business Review*, July–August 1992.

Summary

Leadership and strategy have, as we have seen, important consequences for the way a business is organised and for the quality of goods and services that are produced.
We look further at organisation and quality tomorrow.

Organisational change and the quality movement

In the last three decades, the marketplace has changed from a state of stability and uniformity to one of volatility and variety. In order to respond to this environment, organisations have had to make radical changes. The upsurge of interest in quality management has also resulted in organisational change; this is principally because quality has come – a message reinforced by all the quality gurus – to signify a commitment to improving the ways things are done.

Today, we shall look at the gurus who have helped to shape this new world of organisations.

1 *Organisational change:*

- Tom Peters
- Charles Handy
- Rosabeth Moss Kanter
- R. Meredith Belbin
- Michael Hammer
- Edgar Schein
- Geert Hofstede

2 *The quality movement:*

- W. E. Deming
- Joseph Juran
- Philip Crosby

Organisational change

In this area, the gurus have focused on organisational
flexibility, empowerment, employability, teamworking,
organisational and national cultures, and process
management.

Tom Peters – Thriving on Chaos

Tom Peters (b. 1942) is an American who spent several
years at the management consultancy company McKinsey
before becoming a writer and lecturer. Although he has
never worked as a manager (he describes himself as an
observer and analyst), he has a widespread knowledge of
organisations, and in recent times has had perhaps the
greatest impact of all the gurus.

In Search of Excellence, co-written with Robert Waterman,
identified a number of excellent companies and drew out
a number of lessons from their experience which can be
applied universally to big and small companies alike.
Although many of these companies are no longer
successful, the eight characteristics of excellent companies
which Peters and Waterman identified are still
acknowledged to be important.

1 A bias for action.
2 Close to the customer.
3 Autonomy and entrepreneurship.
4 Productivity through people.
5 Hands-on value driven (executives make things
   happen).

6 Stick to the knitting.
7 Simple form and a lean staff.
8 Simultaneous loose–tight properties (controlled and empowered; big yet small).

Liberation management concentrated on organisation structure, again looking to individual companies for examples. Peters argued that organisations should be lean, flat and flexible so that they can transform themselves rapidly to respond to the swift pace of change. This is helped by a willingness to innovate and to focus on customers. In such structures, managers need new skills which emphasise the softer rather than the harder side of management.

Peters has a knack of tuning into the prevailing trends and issues and responding to these at the right time. Some critics accuse him of inconsistency, but others argue that an ability to shift one's attitude and position is necessary in an era of rapid change. Peters is now turning his attention to the individual.

Key texts: *In Search of Excellence*, 1982; *Thriving on Chaos*, 1989; *Liberation Management*, 1992.

Charles Handy – Discontinuous Change

Charles Handy (b. 1932) is a writer and broadcaster, born in Ireland. He worked in industry before joining academia, later becoming Visiting Professor at the London Business School. His first book, *Understanding Organizations* (1976), is a comprehensive study which has become a standard work for managers and students alike.

In *The Age of Unreason* (1989), Handy identifies three organisational forms of the future.

1 *The Shamrock Organisation* – the three leaves of the shamrock are the core workers, the contractual fringe and the flexible labour force. This model was developed later in *The Empty Raincoat* (1994) where Handy used the metaphor of *the inverted doughnut:* permanent workers form the core whilst the substance of the doughnut is filled by contract and flexible workers.

2 *The Federal Organisation* – this works on the principle that key activities within an organisation operate as distinct units but ally together and take a shared identity. The principle of subsidiarity is important. Federalism can only work where the centre surrenders power to the units (Peters' loose–tight properties) and where its main role is to coordinate and advise.

3 *The Triple I Organisation* – this consists of intelligence, information and ideas.

Handy is concerned with individuals as much as with organisations. He argues that the three structures can only work properly when organisations are prepared to trust and invest in their workers. He developed the concept of *portfolio working* where full-time work will be a thing of the past. Most recently, Handy has become a proponent and practitioner of *downshifting*, a philosophy of life where people work and earn less but enjoy a greater quality of life. His latest book looks at the effects of the competitive ethos of capitalism on individuals. If competition is pushed too far, he warns, people become stressed and also selfish, subjective and insensitive. He warns that this is as bad for business as it is for personal relationships.

Handy's messages can be uncomfortable, and have been criticised for being unrealistic. However, by the sheer readability of his writing and his intriguing use of analogy, metaphor and anecdote, he stands apart from many other management writers. He is not merely an observer and commentator on change but also a catalyst who forces people to stand outside the routine of the day-to-day and acknowledge change and address its implications.

Key texts: *Understanding Organizations*, 1976; *The Age of Unreason*, 1989; *The Empty Raincoat*, 1994; *The Hungry Spirit*, 1997.

Ricardo Semler is a Brazilian who, in 1980, took over the ailing Semco, the family firm, from his father. He turned it around using the three main strategies of employee democracy, profit sharing and open information systems. Semler's way of running an organisation seems radical to some, but his practice has reflected what the gurus have suggested. In *Maverick!* (1993) he explains his philosophy: 'To survive in modern times, a company must have an organizational structure that accepts change as its basic premise, lets tribal customs thrive, and fosters a power that is derived from respect, not rules. In other words, the successful companies will be the ones that put quality of life first.'

Rosabeth Moss Kanter – Empowerment

Rosabeth Moss Kanter (b. 1943) is an American sociologist, consultant, lecturer and a Professor at Harvard Business School. She, like Charles Handy, is interested in new organisational models and has also attempted to focus senior management's attention on people within organisations. She was one of the first writers to encourage managers to energise and *empower* their people. Her aim was to help executives stay ahead of change rather than to become victims of it. She provided a blueprint for successful harnessing of change, giving rules both for encouraging innovation and building commitment.

In *When Giants Learn to Dance*, she recognises, like Handy, that as companies concentrate on their core capabilities, expansion will occur through strategic alliances and peripheral activities will be outsourced. She identifies skills which managers must learn in order to be flexible in the 'post-entrepreneurial corporation' where 'relationships and communication and the flexibility to temporarily combine resources are more important than the "formal" channels and reporting relationships represented on an organisational chart.' She advocates building structures around small autonomous teams where people are encouraged to be enterprising and use their problem-solving abilities.

Moss Kanter's work can be seen as a development of earlier research by Mayo and McGregor which studied the relationship between the individual and the organisation. Although she has been criticised for depending too much on the idea that corporate growth will come from an emphasis on people, her contribution is that she continued to stress the importance of the people side of management in the late 1980s and the first half of the 1990s – an era of cost-cutting and redundancies. Her latest work looks at the impact of globalisation on local communities and on the people who work for world-class companies.

Key texts: *The Change Masters: Corporate Entrepreneurs at Work*, 1983; *When Giants Learn to Dance*, 1989; *Becoming World Class*, 1996.

R. Meredith Belbin – Team Role Theory

R. Meredith Belbin (b. 1926) is an English academic who has also spent periods working in industry and now has his own consultancy company. As a result of research carried out at Henley Management College in the 1970s, he discovered eight (later extended to nine) useful roles which are necessary for a successful team:

1 Plant.
2 Coordinator.
3 Shaper.
4 Teamworker.
5 Completer.
6 Implementer.
7 Resource investigator.
8 Specialist.
9 Monitor evaluator.

The essence of Belbin's theory is that, given the knowledge of the abilities and characteristics of individual team members, success or failure can be predicted within certain limits. As a result, unsuccessful teams can be improved by analysing their shortcomings and making changes. A self-perception inventory is included in *Management Teams* as a quick and easy way for managers to work out what their own team roles should be. In response to criticism that this is too subjective for organisational use, Belbin later developed a computerised system called Interplace.

There has been an enduring interest in team role categories on the part of practising managers, partly because of the increasing interest in teamworking in the 1980s and 1990s. Belbin was the first to develop our understanding of the dynamics of teams, which is seen as a key ingredient in individual and organisational learning.

Key text: *Management Teams: Why They Succeed or Fail*, 1980.

Michael Hammer – Re-engineering

No other concept has recently received more interest and criticism than re-engineering. This is because it is a concept which is easy to understand but difficult to put into practice.

Michael Hammer (b. 1948) is a former computer-science professor at the Massachusetts Institute of Technology and now runs his own consulting firm. Re-engineering was not Hammer's original idea but he popularised it, defining it in *Re-engineering the Corporation*, which he wrote with James Champy, as 'the fundamental rethinking and radical redesign of business processes to achieve dramatic improvements in critical contemporary measures of performance, such as cost, quality, service and speed'. He suggested that successful re-engineering projects are founded on six basic principles.

1 Organise around outcomes not tasks.
2 Have those who produce the output of the process perform the process.
3 Subsume information-processing into the real work that produces the information.
4 Treat geographically dispersed resources as though they were centralised.

> 5 Link parallel activities instead of integrating their tasks.
> 6 Put the decision point where work is performed, and build control into the process.

In spite of a few well-known examples of success, there is much evidence to suggest that re-engineering fails or at best produces only marginal results in the majority of organisations in which it is implemented. In some organisations, this is due to the fact that the programmes are not sufficiently radical, only tinkering with the most easily accessible processes. In others, it is because the human side is not managed sensitively and re-engineering is used as a cover for making redundancies. Hammer is now looking at supply chain re-engineering which means changing not only a firm's internal operations but also how it interacts with its customers and suppliers – shades of Porter's Value Chain.

Key texts: 'Re-engineering work: don't automate, obliterate', *Harvard Business Review*, July–August 1990; *Re-engineering the Corporation* (with James Champy), 1993.

Edgar Schein – Corporate Culture

Edgar Schein (b. 1928) is a social psychologist who is now Professor of Management at the Sloan School of Management at the Massachusetts Institute of Technology. The early development of his work was shaped by thinkers such as McGregor, Bennis and Argyris, and he in turn has influenced others such as Charles Handy. Schein looks at culture from a number of perspectives, particularly its relationship to leadership and its role in organisational change.

He defines culture as a pattern of basic assumptions, which are constantly changing, learned by a given group. Organisation culture has three main elements:

1 *Artefacts* – the physical layout, office landscape and dress code.
2 *Values* – principles upon which people base their behaviour.
3 *Underlying assumptions* – sources of values and beliefs.

If there is to be an alignment of culture with strategy, there has to be a large measure of consensus among employees and managers concerning:

- *The core mission or primary task* – what business are we in?
- *Goals* – what should we do?
- *Strategy* – means of accomplishing goals
- *Progress* – how do we measure it?
- *Remedial strategies* – what do we do when things go wrong?

Schein invented the term *psychological contract* (although he attributes the origins of the concept to Argyris – see Thursday) which he defined in *Organizational Psychology* (1980) as 'an unwritten set of expectations operating at all times between every member of an organization and the various managers and others in that organization'. Schein also looked at individuals' varying aspirations and motivations. His key finding is that, once mature, they have one main so-called career anchor, the underlying career value which they are unwilling to surrender.

Key texts: *Organizational Culture and Leadership*, 1985;
Career Anchors: Discovering Your Real Values, 1990.

Geert Hofstede – Dimensions of National Culture

Geert Hofstede (b. 1928) is a Dutch academic who has
spent periods in industry, including IBM, and is Emeritus
Professor of Organisational Anthropology and International
Management at the University at Limburg at Maastricht.
He is a pioneer of research on national cultures and their
effects on business.

Hofstede identified four dimensions associated with
national culture in *Cultures and Organizations:*

1 *Power/distance* – 'the extent to which the less
   powerful members of institutions and organizations
   within a country expect and accept that power is
   distributed unequally.'
2 *Individualism/collectivism* – 'Individualism pertains to
   societies in which ties between individuals are loose:
   everyone is expected to look after himself or herself
   and his or her immediate family. Collectivism as its
   opposite pertains to societies in which people from
   birth onwards are integrated into strong, cohesive
   ingroups, which throughout people's lifetime continue
   to protect them in exchange for unquestioning loyalty.'
3 *Masculinity/femininity* – 'Masculinity pertains to
   societies in which social gender roles are clearly
   distinct; femininity pertains to societies in which
   social gender roles overlap.'

> 4 *Uncertainty avoidance* – 'The extent to which the
> members of a culture feel threatened by uncertain
> or unknown situations.'

Hofstede is keen to emphasise that these dimensions are
not prescriptive but merely a framework for helping us
manage cultural diversity in an age of global business.

Other researchers have extended this work, discovering
a fifth dimension: *long-term/short-term* orientation. This
measures the extent to which a country takes a long- or short-
term view of life. Fons Trompenaars has carried out extensive
research which shows how national culture influences
corporate culture, identifying four types of corporate culture
which are comparable with Hofstede's model. These are:

> 1 The Family – a power-oriented culture.
> 2 The Eiffel Tower – a role-oriented culture.
> 3 The Guided Missile – a project-oriented culture.
> 4 The Incubator – a fulfilment-oriented culture.

Key texts: Hofstede: *Culture's Consequences: International
Differences in Work-related Values*, 1980; Hofstede: *Cultures
and Organizations: Software of the Mind*, 1991; Trompenaars:
Riding the Waves of Culture, 1993.

The quality movement

The quality movement has found its most influential
expression in Total Quality Management, a philosophical
approach to organisational development which constantly
focuses the efforts of every employee on maintaining and
improving an organisation's services or products.

W. Edwards Deming – The Father of the Quality Movement

W. Edwards Deming (1900–1993) was working in the US National Bureau of the Census when he observed that statistical techniques for ensuring quality control were adequate for correcting defects but inadequate for improving the ways things were done. Unless the process was changed, the mistake would be continually repeated.

The core of Deming's philosophy was that in order to improve the quality of production over time, the people doing the job have to be involved in the improvement of the production process. Deming argued that employees' intellect and sense of responsibility have to participate in the quality process as well as their physical effort. The key component in this exercise of winning worker commitment consists of teams sharing a vision of continuous improvement.

After the war, Deming was sent to Japan as an adviser in census techniques. His ideas were more enthusiastically received by the war-torn and resource-depleted Japanese than in the American boom market where anything that was produced was sold.

Deming's philosophy is succinctly summarised in his famous 14 Points, where he stated the case for the abolition of constricting performance appraisals, performance-related pay, productivity quotas and bonuses, in favour of continuous training on the job, education and self-improvement programmes, breaking down barriers between departments, driving out fear so that people could work effectively, and removing all barriers that robbed people of their right to pride of workmanship.

Deming has been criticised for his approach to performance appraisal and his dismissal of management by objectives, but he is credited with an enormous contribution to the thinking behind the post-war Japanese economic miracle.

Key text: *Out of the Crisis*, 1986.

Joseph M. Juran – 'There is Gold in the Mine'

'There is gold in the mine' is a phrase coined by Joseph M. Juran (b. 1904) to signify the potentially large cost savings to be made by identifying and solving quality problems.

A Balkan-born American, Juran started his professional life as an engineer, and like Deming was invited to lecture in Japan. Juran believes that as few as 20 per cent of quality problems can be attributed to shop-floor workers and that the quality breakthrough lies in the attitudes of managers. Quality control should be conducted as an integral part of management control. As most organisations are unaware of the price they are paying for doing things wrong, he used cost quantification of quality problems to sensitise management to the issues of quality.

Juran believes that quality does not happen by accident. Planning comes first in his quality trilogy: planning, control and improvement. The key elements he identifies in implementing company-wide strategic quality planning have since become standard features of business planning: identifying customer needs, interpreting those needs and designing products to meet them, optimising product features so as to meet the organisation's as well as the customer's needs, developing and optimising processes to produce the products, testing the process thoroughly and making it operational.

Like Deming, Juran has been critical of senior Western management, and his stance is largely one of trying to overcome a negative approach through emphasis on training and top management leadership.

Key text: *Juran on Planning for Quality*, 1988.

Philip B. Crosby – Quality is Free; Do it Right First Time; Zero Defects

Philip Crosby (b. 1926) was Corporate Vice President and Director of Quality for ITT for 14 years. In 1979, he wrote *Quality is Free* which became a best-seller. In 1991, he retired from Philip Crosby Associates to launch Career IV, Inc to help develop senior executives.

For Crosby, quality means conformance to requirements which the company establishes from knowledge of its customers' needs. Good or bad, high or low quality are all meaningless to Crosby. Quality measurement is the price of non-conformance – the cost of not doing it right first time. Crosby has estimated that systems which allow things to go wrong so that they have to be done again can cost organisations between 20–35 per cent of their revenues.

Quality improvement is a process which requires determination and education as well as implementation.

Crosby's 14 steps to quality improvement include management commitment, cross-departmental improvement teams, evaluation of the cost of quality, raising quality awareness among all employees, action for correcting problems, monitoring progress and training supervisors.

Crosby argues that some organisations can compound quality problems by using thoughtless or unconcerned ways of managing people. He encourages individuals to establish improvement goals and to communicate any problems or obstacles to management. His later work reflects a broader approach to improvement, and he defines five elements essential to becoming an eternally successful organisation.

1 People routinely do things right first time.
2 Change is anticipated and used to advantage.
3 Growth is consistent and profitable.
4 New products and services appear when needed.
5 Everyone is happy to work there.

Key texts: *Quality is Free*, 1979; *Quality Without Tears*, 1984; *The Eternally Successful Organisation*, 1988.

'At Xerox, we're very keen on empowering people and unleashing their creative juices – and we see processes as liberating. After all, if you have processes that are in control, you know how the organization is working. There's no guesswork because variances are small and operating limits are well defined. Couple that with objectives that are consistent with your strategy and communicated all the way down the line – to individuals on the production floor as well as to those who deal directly with customers – and you get quality output without a lot of checking. You don't need the old command-and-control approach, which was designed to keep people in line; instead you can tell people to do their own thing provided they respect the process. You wind up with an environment that frees people to be creative. This connection to empowerment turned out to be critical for us: if people don't understand it, they tend to resist a process approach because they think it will restrict their creativity. But it does exactly the opposite.'

Source: Paul Allaire, chairman and CEO of Xerox, quoted in 'Leveraging processes for strategic advantage', David A. Garvin, *Harvard Business Review,* September–October 1995.

Summary

The twin commitments to managing people so that they give of their best and to working towards continuous improvement have evolved into an aspiration towards organisational learning. This we look at tomorrow.

Learning

At the end of the 20th century, individual and organisational learning is increasingly seen as the major competitive weapon in facing up to change. Creating a climate for learning and the right conditions for self-motivation so that the organisation continues to change and develop forms the subject of ever-expanding experimentation and writing.

We shall focus on:

- The Tavistock Institute
- Reg Revans
- David McClelland
- David Kolb
- Peter Honey and Alan Mumford
- Chris Argyris
- Peter Senge
- Stephen Covey

The Tavistock Institute

Much of the early work on learning evolved from human-relations thinking and was carried out by the Tavistock Institute. This was set up in the UK in 1947 to examine how organisations respond to change in their environment, and to study the psychological and social forces affecting group behaviour. Researchers in the Tavistock Institute recognised that a Taylorist approach was ineffectual in tackling change because systems broke down where human interaction and contribution were nullified. They were amongst the first to recognise that organisational systems should not reduce jobs to the lowest common denominator, but should rather develop them so as to embrace greater variety and skills so that people could motivate themselves to higher performance.

Research by the Institute led to a view of managers, not as issuers of instructions, but as teachers delegating decisions and developing skills.

Reg Revans – Action Learning

In the business of industrial development and education, Reg Revans (b. 1907) scorned formal classroom teaching and argued that the best kind of learning is that which happens in the workplace by those who do the jobs. Revans researched the behaviour of miners and found them ill-equipped to handle formalised educational methods but highly effective when left to work out their own solutions.

For Revans, the best learning is on-the-job where small groups tackle real problems through a process of 'questioning insight'. He argued that organisations should give people the scope to learn both for themselves and from each other. This should occur by getting them to focus not on simulations or case studies but on live problems by keeping simple yet penetrating questions at the forefront of their thinking in tackling problems, change and improvement.

Revans said that by asking him- or herself how things went today, the manager ought, without great difficulty, to contrive that they go better tomorrow. He understood that an organisation creates obstacles to development through the remoteness of decision-making from the workplace. Revans saw the manager not as a teacher who imparts knowledge but as a facilitator who helps, steers and guides the group to work towards its own solutions.

Although Revans' work was largely ignored by his academic contemporaries, his method of Action Learning has now been widely applied throughout the world. This was done with particular success in Belgium in the 1970s and 1980s when national output surpassed that of many major competitors. His approach has also evolved into other learning theories.

Key text: *Action Learning: New Techniques for Management*, 1980.

David McClelland – Competence

In the 1990s, learning in the workplace – as opposed to the classroom – has mushroomed into a major industry with vocational qualifications based on the concept of competence. One early influence was Stephen Boyatzis, but the term had actually started to take on earlier significance with a Harvard psychology professor, David McClelland, (b. 1920), in 1973.

Like Revans, McClelland argued that traditional academic examinations did not predict or nurture effectiveness in job performance.

AN EXCELLENT HONOURS DEGREE, MR JONES. NOW WHAT CAN YOU ACTUALLY DO?

McClelland sought other variables or characteristics which cause effective or superior performance in a job; these he called competencies – motives, skills or a body of knowledge that the individual puts to use.

Attainment of competence is at the root of the UK's National Management Occupational Standards which are used as a basis for curriculum development, or alternatively for job and people specifications. With the work of Prahalad and Hamel, as we saw on Tuesday, the notion of core competencies has also evolved at organisational level.

Key texts: McClelland: 'Testing for competence rather than intelligence', *American Psychologist*, vol. 28, 1973; Boyatzis: *The Competent Manager: a Model for Effective Performance*, 1982.

David Kolb – Experiential Learning

The research of David Kolb (b. 1939) into experiential learning at Case Western Reserve University, Cleveland, Ohio, has been enormously influential in providing a simple model of how adults learn.

In order to set Kolb's work into context, think back to how you learned to swim or to ride a bike. You might find it hard to remember how you tentatively got on the bike, tried to pedal, fell off and thought 'I'm not doing that again!' You think a bit and try again, trying something slightly differently this time and so on, rejecting or avoiding certain motions and trying and adopting those which seem to work better.

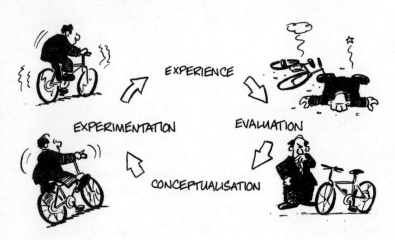

For Kolb, learning is a cycle which generally starts with *experience* and then moves on to *evaluation* of that experience to *conceptualise* and improve the way of doing things which requires further *experimentation*. At the centre of this deceptively simple approach is the notion that we learn to do things by trying them out. At each stage of the cycle, the individual picks up a different kind of knowledge.

Key text: *Experiential Learning: Experience as the Source of Learning and Development*, 1984.

> *'If you expect people to be able to operate more than a till, you need to educate them on the issues and enable them to challenge what's going on in the workplace. ... All the best education is experiential ... you can't change people's minds and ways of thinking unless you change their experiences. ... The vision of this company is to create business more for the public good than for private greed and we therefore have to challenge directors without fear of reprisal and in knowledge that they will be listened to. Most companies are run like hierarchies and God help them if you challenge them.'*
>
> Source: Anita Roddick on The Body Shop, quoted in 'Daring to be different', *Management Training*, February 1993.

Peter Honey and Alan Mumford – Learning Styles

Kolb hypothesised and tested various learning styles or approaches because different people have different levels of comfort or difficulty in relation to various phases of this cycle of experience – evaluation – conceptualisation – experimentation. But it is the work of Honey and Mumford which has had a widespread impact in understanding that there is no prescriptive, universal formula; that we all have our own preferred learning style.

Peter Honey is an independent chartered psychologist and like Alan Mumford is a Visiting Professor at the International Management Centres, Buckingham.

Following on from Revans' 'learning to learn by doing' and Kolb's emphasis on reflecting on experience, Honey and Mumford have identified four basic types of learner.

1 *Activists* who like to get involved in new experiences, enjoy the adrenalin of things chopping and changing as part of a team, and tend to enjoy high visibility.

2 *Theorists* who like to question assumptions and methodologies and learn best when they have the time to explore links between ideas and situations.

3 *Pragmatists* who are all for practicality. They learn best when there is a link between the subject matter and the job in hand, and from opportunities where they can try out what they have learned.

4 *Reflectors* who like to take their time and think things through. They learn best from activities where they can watch, observe and carry out research.

Honey and Mumford point out that most of us are a mix of these learning styles. It would be unusual to find someone who is exclusively a reflector, for example, but not unusual to find that some people are more reflector than they are activist, or more theorist than they are pragmatist.

Honey's and Mumford's work continues to be widely applied today in helping to understand individual behaviour in a group context and in building balanced groups or teams.

Key text: *Manual of Learning Styles*, 1982 and revisions.

Chris Argyris – Double-Loop Learning

A psychologist based at Harvard, Chris Argyris (b. 1923) follows a different route from McClelland and Kolb by focusing on organisational learning. While it is the individuals who actually do the learning, Argyris argues that the organisation can inhibit learning because it imposes – perhaps unconsciously – rules over the ways in which people relate to each other. Argyris says that problem-solving and decision-making can be dominated by an almost unconscious drive to 'save face', 'protect others' and maintain the status quo. Rather than tackle the big questions such as why problems arise in the first place, Argyris says that managers are increasingly conditioned to go for a cure – a quick fix which may treat a particular situation (e.g. develop a customer-retention complaints programme) – rather than prevention – i.e. solving the real problem (e.g. why is there a regular flow of complaints? Where do these come from? And more importantly, what are we *really* going to do about putting the situation right?).

For Argyris, there are two ways of tackling problems:

1 *Single-loop learning* addresses superficial symptoms and outcomes. This approach is one-dimensional in that although it treats the problem, it does not make it go away.
2 *Double-loop learning* goes further by questioning why the problem arose in the first place and probes ways of preventing the problem by searching for ways of changing the way things are done. It is double-loop learning which creates real change and improvement.

Argyris says that successful adoption of double-loop learning is a quantum leap which can take a long time because it will forcibly change our reasoning, attitudes and the organisation's culture. His research continues to tackle unintentional dishonesty in organisations as the greatest obstacle to organisational learning.

Key texts: *Organizational Learning – A Theory of Action Perspective* (with David Schon), 1978; 'Good communication that blocks learning', *Harvard Business Review*, July–August 1994.

Peter Senge - The Learning Organisation

Peter Senge (b. 1948), Head of the Centre for Organisational Learning at Massachussetts Institute of Technology, has been described as Mr Learning Organisation. For Senge, the key to understanding how organisations work lies in how people think and interact. Organisations cannot change unless people change the way they think.

In the learning organisation, old organisational – i.e. command and control – thinking is replaced with the adoption of Senge's five new component technologies: mental models, personal mastery, systems thinking, shared vision and team learning. Senge argues that people should shed their old ways of thinking (mental models), learn to be open with others (personal mastery), understand how the organisation really works (systems thinking), create goals and plans that everyone subscribes to (shared visions) and then work together to achieve those goals (team learning).

For Senge, the learning organisation signifies the capacity to shift away from views inherent in a traditional, hierarchical organisation towards the ability of everyone to challenge prevailing thinking, bring unofficial networks of thinking to the surface, see the bigger picture and gain a balanced perspective of the short and long term.

Essentially, the learning organisation means the collective ability to develop shared visions which capture and exploit people's willingness, commitment and curiosity. Senge believes that people will be sufficiently motivated by the organisational vision, if it is positive enough, using what he calls 'creative tension' to suggest, argue, innovate and propose ways forward. Creative tension can be seen as an outcome of Revans' questioning insight and Argyris' probing questioning. The only people who can make learning really happen are managers themselves.

Senge's work has been criticised as unnecessarily obscure, although his thinking enjoys a wide influence.

Key text: *The Fifth Discipline – the Art and Practice of the Learning Organisation*, 1990.

Stephen Covey – Self First

The major theme of the gurus we have looked at today focuses on the individual's capacity to learn in an organisational context. The research and writing of Stephen Covey pushes the focus back onto the individual to an extreme which can be traced back to the self-help ethic of Samuel Smiles and the positive self-drive of Dale Carnegie who advised us 'how to win friends and influence people'.

Covey is a practising mormon whose lectures at Brigham Young University in the 1980s attracted students in their thousands. In 1985 he set up the Covey Leadership Centre. His message was attractive enough for President Bill Clinton to invite him to Camp David. His book, described by Warren Bennis as remarkable, has sold over 5 million copies.

Covey's research into American success literature led him to conclude that superficial skills were no panacea for success in a world where people were being re-engineered out of jobs. His answer was that people should get back to the harsher disciplines of self-awareness and character-building.

Covey's seven habits are divided into three sections:
private victory, public victory and renewal.

- *Private victory:*

  1 *Be proactive* – the principle of personal vision.
  2 *Begin with the end in mind* – the principle of
    personal leadership.
  3 *Put first things first* – the principle of
    self-management.

  Learning and understanding the habits of private
  victory will help the individual to gain increased
  self-confidence, to know the self in a deeper, more
  meaningful way and to grow a sense of identity,
  integrity and control.

- *Public victory:*

  4 *Think Win/Win* – the principle of interpersonal
    leadership.
  5 *Seek first to understand, then to be understood* –
    the principles of empathic communication.
  6 *Synergise* – the principles of creative cooperation.

  The habits of public victory help to heal and rebuild
  important relationships that have deteriorated or
  broken; good relationships will improve, become
  deeper and more creative.

- *Renewal:*

  7 *Sharpen the saw* – the principles of balanced
    self-renewal.

The seventh habit renews the first six and leads to real independence and effective interdependence.

Commentators have both criticised and acclaimed Covey's approach for mixing the self-help message and current management theories with religious fervour for application to the character, even the soul. At the time of writing, however, Coveyism is expanding and reflects a message which promises to gain wider recognition and to continue to grow.

Key text: *The Seven Habits of Highly Effective Managers: Restoring the Character Ethic*, 1989.

Summary

If Covey has looked to the past for sources of inspiration for a difficult present, where should we look for the future? We speculate on the next generation of gurus tomorrow.

The next generation

So who will be the next management gurus? Where will they come from, and what will their message be? Today, we revisit the themes which we have traced from Monday through to Thursday and speculate on the future.
In considering the work of:

- Bruce Tulgan
- Robert Kaplan and David Norton
- Richard Pascale
- Christopher Barnatt
- Arie de Geus
- Gareth Morgan
- Ikujiro Nonaka

we look at potential extensions of work measurement and control, at the organisation developing into new forms, aided by flexibility, virtuality and knowledge management, and at creativity and the individual.

We look first at tomorrow's workforce, something which has been described by Bruce Tulgan as Generation X.

Bruce Tulgan – Generation X

The concept of Generation X – the notion that today's young people are different from those who have come before them and are adopting a different approach to work – has captured widespread attention. It is the brainchild of Bruce Tulgan (b. 1967), an ex-lawyer and founder of the consultancy Rainmaker. Generation X, he argues, has been created by invasive media, worldwide consumer products, the decline of trust and the realisation that self-reliance is the only sure thing in an age of uncertainty. The younger generation – the Xers – are characterised by a constant search for variety and a fear of boredom, the desire to learn, the demand for honesty and the tacit acceptance of gender equality. Managing this group requires a new implicit contract based around learning opportunities and creative responsibility. Xers are not rejecting institutions, however, institutions are rejecting Xers.

Critics retort that all this is no more than the youthful expression of youth itself, and that, deep down, there are no fundamental differences between 'them' and 'us'. It is difficult to know whether this concept has lasting significance, but it reflects many of the trends of the 1990s, in particular the renegotiation of Schein's psychological contract.

Tulgan is currently researching into career structures in the workplace of the future.

Key text: *Managing Generation X: How to Bring Out the Best in Young Talent*, 1995.

We can assume that traces of Taylorism will not go away in the future. It has been prevalent for nearly 100 years and remanifests itself today in re-engineering, quality systems, benchmarking and performance measurement. It is difficult to conceive, therefore, of the future of work without some form of analysis, measurement and control despite the attraction of approaches such as Ricardo Semler's (see Wednesday) which takes apparently *laissez-faire* management to new – and successful – heights.

Robert Kaplan and David Norton – The Balanced Scorecard

The Balanced Scorecard – one of the latest models for measuring business performance – looks at intangible assets, such as customer satisfaction, alongside traditional financial measures. It was proposed in a 1992 *Harvard Business Review* article by Robert Kaplan, Professor of Accounting at Harvard Business School, and David Norton, President of the consulting firm Renaissance Strategy Group, with the saying 'What you measure is what you get'. They argued that organisations need realistic measures which are meaningful to employees, relate visibly to strategic direction and provide a balanced picture of what is happening throughout the organisation, not just in one facet of it. The Balanced Scorecard concentrates on four strategic areas:

1 Financial measures.
2 Customer measures.
3 Internal business process measures.
4 Learning and innovation measures.

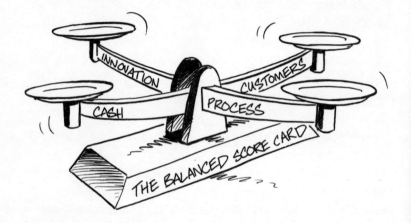

Although on first sight the Balanced Scorecard is simple
and flexible, it can be complex to implement in practice.
An increasing number of organisations are trying out the
Balanced Scorecard, however: Norton claims that
60 per cent of large American companies are using
some sort of variation which combines financial with
non-financial measures.

Key text: *The Balanced Scorecard: Translating Strategy into
Action*, 1996.

The organisation itself will continue to seek out new forms
and structures. We have moved a long way – in theory at
least – from the command and control pyramid of Fayol
and Weber to the newer networking capability emerging

out of the convergence of computing and telecommunications in the Virtual Organisation. As organisations continue to diversify, re-engineer themselves, decentralise and break up, it would be astounding if an army of experts is wrong and small business does not provide a model for the future. Will Professor E. F. Schumacher (1911–1977), author of *Small is Beautiful*, re-emerge as one of the gurus of the future, or will organisational form and structure take different directions?

Richard Pascale – Agility

In *The Art of Japanese Management*, Richard Pascale, formerly of Stanford, now an Associate Fellow at Oxford University, concluded that the success of Japanese companies could be attributed to the way that they adopted the McKinsey Seven-S strategy framework, the model in which shared values linked strategy, systems and skills to management style and staffing needs. Pascale's interest in the way organisations adapt and perform has developed further into four key concepts.

1 *Power* – can employees really influence the course of corporate events?
2 *Identity* – do individuals identify with the organisation as a whole?
3 *Contention* – how is conflict brought out and used creatively?
4 *Learning* – how does the organisation handle and develop new ideas?

For Pascale, positive answers to these questions are the vital signs of *agility* – the core competence of the future which may arrest organisations from atrophying into complacency. Many writers – Peters, Senge and Covey among them – agree that agility means discomfort and facing up to what was previously brushed under the carpet. Harnessing dissent is all part of the process to deal with the real people issues which impede creativity and progress.

Key texts: *The Art of Japanese Management* (with Anthony G. Athos), 1981; *Managing on the Edge: How Successful Companies use Conflict to Stay Ahead*, 1990.

Christopher Barnatt – The Virtual Organisation

The concept of the Virtual Organisation is not immediately straightforward to grasp. Basically, virtuality embraces a range of flexible working practices facilitated by new communications technologies. Companies come to see themselves not as fixed structures but as networks of resources to be assembled and disassembled according to market need and irrespective of physical location. No single writer can be said to 'own' the concept of *virtuality*, but Christopher Barnatt, at the School of Management and Finance, University of Nottingham, has written more – and more consistently – about this, and a similar term, *cyberbusiness*, than many. He tackles the new mix of technology, organisation structure and the place of people, and attempts to predict the implications for the future.

Key text: *Cyberbusiness: Mindsets for a Wired Age*, 1995.

Arie de Geus – Corporate Longevity

Arie de Geus, a former strategist for Royal Dutch Shell, and Visiting Professor at the London Business School, identifies what he calls *living companies*. These are in fact long-lived companies whose longevity does not depend on their ability to maximise immediate returns to shareholders or on the country or industry in which they operate. It has rather to do with four particular characteristics.

1. *Financial conservatism.*
2. *Sensitivity* – being tuned to the environment and adapting accordingly.
3. *Cohesion* – a strong sense of identity, based on a strong corporate culture.
4. *Tolerance* – to allow employees time to come up with ideas.

De Geus is keen to emphasise that an organisation is a community of human beings that is in business to stay alive.

Many companies fail because they focus too heavily on the side of economics. He argues that the manager of a living company must let people grow within a community that is held together by clearly stated values. To do this, the manager must:

- Value people, not assets
- Respect innovation, not devotion to policy
- Organise for learning rather than for orderly procedures
- Endeavour to perpetuate the human community before all other concerns

Key text: *The Living Company*, 1997.

It is safe to assume that the importance of the individual will continue to grow. Creating a climate for empowerment, self-motivation and creativity has repercussions for professional development, life-long learning and knowledge which, perhaps, have yet to find their champions.

Gareth Morgan – Creativity

Argyris, Senge and Covey have, as we saw yesterday, encouraged us to rethink our approach to learning and achieving. Gareth Morgan (b. 1943), Research Professor at York University in Toronto, has written about the new styles of organisation and thinking that managers need to develop if they are to be successful in a period of uncertainty. *Imaginization* is about improving abilities to see and understand situations in new ways, finding new images for new ways of organising, creating shared understanding and personal empowerment, and developing capability for continuous self-organisation. Imaginization helps us to rethink our roles as managers and develop fresh approaches to design, planning and change. You cannot create a learning organisation, claims Morgan, but you can enhance people's capabilities to learn and to align their activities in concrete ways.

Morgan's thinking is acclaimed by other gurus; and it may well hold a key to the growing theme of personal and organisational transformation.

Key text: *Imaginization – The Art of Creative Management*, 1993.

Ikujiro Nonaka – Knowledge Management

Ikujiro Nonaka (b. 1935) is Professor of Knowledge at the University of California and Dean of the Department of Knowledge Science at Japan's Advanced Institute of Science and Technology in Hokuriku. He claims that knowledge management is a question not of database creation but rather of tapping the implicit know-how stored in people's brains. He also believes – as a counter to downsizing – that companies need plenty of slack – or tolerance as de Geus refers to it – in order to be creative: employees need time to kick around ideas in order to come up with market-changing products. Too much measurement and too much direct accountability, he argues, will lead to sticking to routine and maintaining the status quo.

Nonaka's ideas have been challenged on the basis that they are not new: Drucker first used the term 'knowledge worker' in the 1950s. He is also criticised for focusing on large, well-established Japanese firms, rather than on small start-ups which are often the best environment for knowledge creation. At a time, however, when organisations are just starting to realise how much experience and corporate memory they have lost in the large-scale cutting of middle management jobs, they are beginning to value intangible assets. Knowledge management appears to be a concept right for its time.

WHO WROTE THAT REPORT ON RESTRUCTURING?

WE RESTRUCTURED HIM.

Other writers on knowledge management have also begun to emerge, such as Thomas Stewart with *Intellectual Capital: the New Wealth of Organisations* (1997) and Stan Davis and Jim Botkin with their enigmatically-titled *Monster Under the Bed: How Business is Mastering the Opportunity of Knowledge for Profit* (1994).

Key text: *The Knowledge-Creating Company* (with Hirotaka Takeuchi), 1995.

Summary

Predicting the future is a notoriously dangerous, but necessary, pastime. Some managers and commentators still feel the need to find the next Drucker, even in a world where uncertainty seems the only certainty and obsolescence erodes the value of ideas only too rapidly. Today, we have looked at possibilities for the future development of ideas that have preoccupied the gurus throughout the twentieth century, by speculating on who will emerge as the source of advice on organisational and individual change.

Tomorrow, we look at the other side of the coin and question whether there will be gurus, as we have known them, in the future. We also discuss the benefits to be gained by studying the gurus of the present and the past.

Getting value from the gurus

*'The important and difficult job is never to find the right answer,
it is to find the right question. For there are few things as useless
– if not as dangerous – as the right answer to the wrong question.'*

Source: Peter Drucker, *The Practice of Management*, 1955

Today, we shall question whether the current industry of
advice can survive in its present form. We shall also ask
what benefit we should expect to get from reading the
gurus. We shall consider:

- The rise of the East
- The impact of the Internet
- The guru-watchers
- Getting value from the gurus

The rise of the East

The few major gurus associated with developments in the
East have come from the West. Deming and Juran apart, the
Japanese economic miracle has been achieved largely
without the help of gurus. The companies which have
achieved phenomenal success in the 1980s have done so on
their own. Although their chief executives have risen in
international stature along with the organisation, Japanese
leaders are not, by and large, writers of books, or involved
in the lecture-circuit, like their counterparts in the West.

Japan, the emerging Tiger economies and China have not yet developed individual gurus but instead as cultures have developed a guiding set of principles. Theirs is a group philosophy which embraces the following concepts:

- Harmony in both social and economic relationships
- The long-term view in business and investment, instead of a continual preoccupation with the bottom-line
- Establishing market share before profit
- An emphasis on personal networks and human relationships
- The incorporation of a cluster of related enterprises within one loose federation or grouping, such as the Japanese *keiretsu* and South Korean *chaebol* models
- Stability in employment
- Consensus between government and business
- State and business investment in education and training

In China, the concept of the family-run business, which is not receptive to outsiders, is also an important factor in the lack of interest in the teachings of management gurus.

Given the economic power of the East and the insularity of their companies, will there be any gurus in the future?

The impact of the Internet

Ideas, trends and themes have much shorter life-spans in the 1990s than did those of the 1960s, 1950s and before. Ideas come and go with ever-greater rapidity as they are adopted, adapted, rejected and replaced, or integrated into practice.

The Internet is further accelerating this process as it provides immediate accessibility to information on a scale hitherto unimagined. With this growing market of information pullers and pushers, it will take an almighty effort of branding (such as has been achieved by Michael Porter, for example) for an idea to become established as the domain of one individual alone, when it can become known, discussed, assimilated and practised around the other side of the world more quickly than ever before.

Gurudom is about comparative longevity in the marketplace, the durability of ideas and the ability to come up with new ones. The Internet – as a medium of information dispersal – may well pose a threat to ownership, speed up the obsolescence factor, create an even greater complexity of ideas and change the influence and impact of the gurus themselves.

The guru-watchers

Guru-watching is now a serious business and may also be a determining factor in how we view gurus in the future.

Books and newspaper articles on gurus continue to multiply. Writers such as Stuart Crainer, with books like *The Ultimate Business Library: 50 Books That Made Management*, and Carol Kennedy, with titles like *Managing With the Gurus: Top Level Guidance on 20 Management Techniques*, have become prominent. But there are others too.

Andrzej Huczynski, Professor of Management at the University of Glasgow Business School, has compiled a powerful analysis of the trends and ideas of the gurus of the twentieth century in *Management Gurus: What Makes Them and How to Become One*. More recently, two writers from *The Economist*, John Micklethwait and Adrian Wooldridge, have written a highly readable criticism of the more recent trends in guru thinking in *The Witch Doctors*.

Even the gurus themselves become guru-watchers. Richard Pascale, author of *The Art of Japanese Management* and *Managing on the Edge*, is a fierce critic of what he calls the 'merry-go-round' of ideas to which organisations fall victim. He has compiled a chart showing that in the last 26 years there have been 25 fads, all of which have been embraced by managers at the time, but which have failed to last more than a year or two. The result, he says, is more akin to organisational chaos than to successful organisational transformation.

Darrell Rigby of Bain and Co. compiles an annual study of management tools and techniques in the attempt to pick the fad from something more lasting and valuable. This enables executives either to make sure that they are not missing anything of value or to bypass something which they might not view as useful.

With slogans and catchphrases designed to capture the attention of executives preoccupied with the bottom-line and shareholder pressure, it is hard, sometimes, to dismiss the criticism that the gurus are pandering to the quick fix.

Getting value from the gurus

We can argue that the critics have done managers, and the gurus themselves, a service in restoring the balance and reminding us that there are no simple, prescriptive answers. Rather, there are theories, approaches and techniques which can be tried out in the constant search for improvement.

Drucker infers that the gurus provide us with an insight into asking the right questions. At the very least, the gurus may confirm – or challenge – our own thinking, question inbuilt assumptions and shed light on some of the key preoccupations of today's organisations.

Management theories must not be grasped as quick fixes or panaceas, but, taken in the context of other ideas, of the external environment and of the internal situation of the company, they can give us food for thought and debate. They offer us a chance to stand back and take stock, and help us to see patterns, or to formalise thinking of which we may, or may not, have already been subconsciously aware.

Success is not born of one idea or scheme alone, but results from a myriad of interacting influences which combine in the right mix, in the right place at the right time. There are no universal applications: what works in the past will not necessarily work in the future, and what works over there will not necessarily work over here. On the whole, the gurus have a perception which enables them to read and respond to the feelings, needs and problems of their own era. A guru's approach is not valid in all situations and in all times.

New ideas need reflection and consideration before implementation and can take years to get to work.

'I'm still really preaching what I was a decade ago. The reason it needs to be said again is that most corporations still haven't listened.'

Rosabeth Moss Kanter, quoted in the *Financial Times*,
24 July 1997.

Companies can be slow to respond. Good ideas turn sour when pushed too far or when applied out of context or without due care and attention to industry, corporate and local circumstances. Gurus' ideas are sometimes widely misunderstood and sometimes used as an excuse for failure. So claims Alan Downs in *Beyond the Looking Glass: Overcoming the Seductive Culture of Corporate Narcissism*, 1997:

'The decline of total quality, reengineering, management by objectives, and many other movements has little to do with their inapplicability or assimilation into the organizational landscape. Rather, it is because their champions were never committed to the basic principles or outcomes, and used the program to advance their personal standing in the organization.'

Summary

The ideas we have described this week have come from many diverse sources but represent only a brief summary of the thinking of the gurus. The work of Drucker, Handy, Hamel *et al.* is often fascinating, particularly when it is accompanied by anecdotes and case studies, which enable us to recognise that our problems are not necessarily new, let alone unique.

We started this week by saying that only about 10 per cent of those who purchased *In Search of Excellence* had probably read it. If you have found that any of the ideas in this book have stimulated even a little curiosity, however, then do go back to the source because there is no real substitute for the original, and, to misquote Juran out of context, there probably will be some gold in the mine.

Index of main entries